WHO NEEDS A FIVERR SUCCESS MANAGER?

YOUR SUCCESS MANAGER IN A BOX

Maddie "FontHaunt" Green

Copyright © 2019 Maddie Green

1st Edition

All rights reserved.

This book is dedicated to all the wonderful people who have helped me on my journey to write! I can't possibly list all of them here, but I'd like to offer special recognition and personal thanks to: TJ, Linda, Jack, Susan, Isabel, Chanthira and family, Monnie, Marilyn W., Ellen P., Laura J. and Deborah C.

Table of Contents

Introduction to the Success Manager Program   5

CHAPTER ONE   12
Success Manager Tips on Skills and Profile   12
CHAPTER TWO   16
Specifics on Profile   16
CHAPTER THREE   20
A More Polished Profile   20
The Success Manager Checklist, Titles   21
CHAPTER FOUR   23
The Success Manager Checklist, Services   23
Categories, Subcategories, Service Types   24
CHAPTER FIVE   26
Success Manager Tips: Gig Descriptions   26
CHAPTER SIX   29
Success Manager Tips: Advanced Gig Descriptions   29
CHAPTER SEVEN   31
Success Manager Tips- Marketing   31
CHAPTER EIGHT   33
Success Manager Advanced Tips - Marketing and Price   33
CHAPTER NINE   37
FAQs and More   37

CHAPTER TEN   39
   Deliveries   39
CHAPTER ELEVEN   46
  Gig Requirements   46
CHAPTER TWELVE   49
  Communication   49
CHAPTER THIRTEEN   53
Can you get a Success Manager? 53
What is the Success Management Team (in the Words of a Fiverr Staff Member): 54
CHAPTER FOURTEEN   55
Do you Need a Success Manager? 55
About the Author   57

Introduction to the Success Manager Program

Do you need a Fiverr success manager? Do you have a Fiverr Success Manager? A significant number of sellers from newbies to Top Rated Sellers don't have one or even know what the term means. What you will get in this e-book is a combination of several things. You'll get information that Fiverr has put out about the Success Manager program, which is still handy because they haven't exactly made it obvious. You'll get much more than that.

Before going into what you'll get in this little book, some readers may not even be aware of the Success Manager program or know what an SM is. In the earliest days of the program, it also appears that some of these were called Account Managers (referring to the management of the chosen seller's account.) For some time some of these staff members called themselves Account Managers while others called themselves Success Managers or SM's. In time, it seemed to stabilize and each was called a Success Manager or SM. In this book, SM will be used often to refer to a Success Manager, so SM and Success Manager are used interchangeably.

One of the first indicators most of us got that there was such a program was in 2016 when a forum user posted a screenshot of an email they had received. It was supposedly from Fiverr, but since phishing and other scams have happened, they assumed it was fake. Here is a transcript of that post.

If you want to skip the emails and generic info about the Program Beginnings, Jump Ahead!

The username of the seller who posted it is omitted for privacy reasons:

May 3, 2016 (Fiverr Official Forum Post)

Today I got this email-

Hello there!
In case we haven't already met, my name is Rachel and I'm a Seller Success Manager, part of Fiverr's Customer Relations team.
I am excited to welcome you to our new program, Seller Success, where you will receive an Account Manager!
As your Seller Success Manager, I will be your dedicated Fiverr representative, keeping an eye on your account to make sure that you are getting the most out of Fiverr including reaching out to you in advance for any marketplace feedback. Any Customer Support requests that you may have will be monitored by me so that we can ensure you are receiving priority service. I will also be available not only via e-mail but also via Skype to talk about new features and order or account questions!
If you would like to join in, I would love to schedule a 10-minute call with on Skype to introduce myself and learn more about what we can do to improve your experience on Fiverr!
I look forward to hearing from you

Anyone got the same email? I haven't heard about it so senior's views on this would be much appreciated.

Cheers

Some forum users were suspicious of this at first. You may notice as mentioned that the words Account Manager and Success Manager were both used which was confusing, and most Fiverr users were accustomed to thinking of Skype as a forbidden thing. In a short time, though, several other sellers admitted publicly or privately that they had received the same or similar emails to their Fiverr-connect email or to their Fiverr inbox. It was soon confirmed that some kind of program had begun, though the sellers chosen seemed to be all types. Some had less than 200 reviews, some had thousands. Some were Top Rated Sellers and some were not. They weren't all from any particular country or region. Not all were 100% fluent in English although it did seem that those chosen were able to communicate in English well enough to benefit from the program. Most of Fiverr is in English, so even though some SM's speak other languages, English proficiency is important. The one exception as of 2019 is Fiver Germany which does have some German-centric offerings, but for the most part, English is the norm.

[*Skip this if you are uninterested in the non-English issue*, but it is true that Fiverr used to have a Spanish-centric platform. They disbanded that platform and it is not available as of this writing. They may re-open it at some point, but even if they do, it's important to improve English skills. You CAN still offer services in other languages like blog articles in Spanish, French, German, etc. You CAN offer translation services. You CAN offer voiceovers in a variety of languages. You just need to be able to communicate and write gig descriptions in English.]

A few things emerged that did connect those chosen. All of them had made some sales and had a fairly high positive rating on their completed orders. It appeared that no one was chosen who had an extremely high cancellation rate (over 75% and perhaps less.) Most, if not all, were level 2 or above although it's possible there are some level one's chosen. If so, we haven't found them. All of those chosen were at least making regular sales though not all were doing incredibly high numbers. There didn't seem to be an obvious connection to how much money they were making per week or month, though as far as we could tell, everyone chosen was making at least enough to be considered regular part-time earners. Most were very active on Fiverr and typically responded to messages in less than 4 hours on a regular basis. Not nearly all were active on the Fiverr forum, so we found those by locating forum users who knew other sellers in their region or who had met other sellers at events. We don't have a clear idea of how many were chosen that weren't active on some kind of Fiverr social media whether it was the LinkedIn group, the Facebook or Twitter pages or the Fiverr blog and forum.

I started to contact various sellers I know to find as many sellers with Success Managers as possible. Most were more than willing to share individual stories and details of what they had learned about the program and the advice they had been given. Much of it was the same across categories and seller types, though some people had detailed information for narrower purposes depending on what they had asked. A few of us started to compile broad information they had been given as well as insider information from Question & Answer sessions sellers had with their individual success managers. Some sellers did a little "spy" work by asking some specific questions that we hoped to learn about. We didn't get everything we wanted since the Success Managers had clearly been told to keep certain things to themselves (or they didn't know) and sometimes we got surprising answers. Even so, we got enough actual answers to make it interesting and we found that not all sellers received exactly the same pop-ups, messages, Skype PM's, etc. Except for one or two oddball results, we found that the answers were reasonably consistent so the majority of this book is a compilation of what we learned.

Who needs a Fiverr Success Manager? Well, as you'll see when you read through, the hints given by SM's are sometimes worded strongly. They've used language that indicates that sellers who follow their advice may get ahead in search results. Sellers who use none of the suggested techniques might be low in search or not appear at all. We can't be sure how true this is, but since it's coming directly from people who are on Fiverr staff, there is a good chance that some or all of the information they give could catapult the chosen sellers ahead. What if you AREN'T a chosen seller? If you are new or a part-timer, there is a chance you could be really serious about Fiverr but lose out because you don't have an SM. Even if you are an established seller and you get more bulk/expensive orders BUT have slower delivery times and fewer in the queue, you may be overlooked in the SM program since the chosen sellers seem to be those who sell and deliver frequently even if the orders are small.

By using the information here, you will know everything that our sellers found out even though you may not have a Success Manager (or SM)of your own, this is your Success Manager in a "box" since we'll give you every detail we can. This book is fresh content compiled from 2016 through early 2019. We hope to give all sellers who read this book a chance to benefit from exactly the same information so that even if you aren't chosen by Fiverr, you can choose your own chance at Success!

If you aren't interested in seeing all of the actual letters we were able to gather, just skip on to Chapter Two. Here we will show copies of multiple letters that sellers received. The earliest seems to have come May 1, 2016, so we assume the program at least went into full action around then. It may be interesting to note how much the SM's emphasize their own importance to sellers and how many benefits sellers would get. It may also be useful to note the difference between various real SM letters.

Here are some that we gathered:

Hello there!
In case we haven't already met, my name is Rachel and I'm a Seller Success Manager, part of Fiverr's Customer Relations team.
*I am excited to welcome you to our **new program, Seller Success,** where **you will receive an Account Manager!***
*As your Seller Success Manager, I will be **your dedicated Fiverr representative, keeping an eye on your account to make sure that you are getting the most out of Fiverr** including reaching out to you in advance for any marketplace feedback. Any **Customer Support requests that you may have will be monitored by me so that we can ensure you are receiving priority service.***
*I will also **be available not only via e-mail but also via Skype** to talk about new features and order or account questions!*
If you would like to join in, I would love to schedule a 10-minute call with on Skype to introduce myself and learn more about what we can do to improve your experience on Fiverr!
I look forward hearing from you

"Hello there!

In case we haven't already met, my name is Noam and I'm a Seller Success Manager, part of Fiverr's Customer Relations team.

*I am excited to **announce our new program, the Fiverr Seller Success Program offered exclusively to a selected group of sellers.** The program's goal is to **help sellers become even more successful on Fiverr** and help them develop their business.*

Benefits of the program:

Dedicated Success Manager

VIP customer support

*Tips and **best practices to** improve quality and **increase sales***

Exclusive analytics and insights *relating to your account*

Interested? All that is left is for you to let me know if you would like to join by replying to this email!

*If you do, **I would like to schedule a 10 minute Skype call** to talk more about how we can work together to make the best out of your experience on Fiverr. **If you would like to communicate via chat or email - that's OK** too!"*

Forum post by user:

Updates Regarding this program. **MY success manager gave me some useful suggestions** regarding my account. We had a 10-minute Skype call. After that, I got one email that was the follow-up email of skype chat regarding recommendations. So basically this program is to help the sellers to get more success.

Another email received by a user who had replied "Yes" but had not received an invite to chat:

"Hello!

I wanted to remind you that you joined our Fiverr Seller Success Program. ***The Fiverr Seller Success Program offered exclusively to a selected group of sellers.*** *We hope to* ***help sellers enhance experience on Fiverr*** *and* ***help them with advantages in search placement as well as profile recommendations*** *to bring success.*

In your recent ticket, I monitored the progress to make sure that you were able to resolve your problem since you now have *VIP customer support.*

I would like to discuss areas relating to your account that may be holding you back. I *would like to schedule a 10 minute Skype call* to talk more about how we can work together to improve your analytics and increase your sales. Please reply and let me know if you plan to remain in the Seller Success program.

So, now that you've seen the potential benefits, this book can become your "Success Manager in a Box" as we share with you all the tips and suggestions that we compiled based on Success Manager responses to users who helped create this book. You can decide for yourself if these ideas are actually beneficial, but at the very least, you won't be in the dark! It may be that if you use the tips in this book, you won't need a Success Manager assigned by Fiverr, you can just use these tips and have the same results!

From here I will take the info gathered by the group and I will list for you all of the tips that were gathered, and when available I'll tell you the reason the SM gave the user relating to why the tip is important. Some of this content will be blended to avoid redundancy and to protect the identity of sellers who chose to help. While a few SM names were listed in the introduction letters, from here the individual names of the Success Managers won't be given.

You can either read this book through just to know what you might be missing, or you can use the summaries at the end of each chapter as a kind of workbook to go through your gigs and implement some or all of the SM ideas.

I was offered transcripts from some of those first and second Skype calls with SM's. Anything that seems useful will be included here, but instead of just listing the transcripts with all the stamps and names, the information will be given according to what it applied to. Some of this will be related to specific Fiverr categories and some of it is broad. Anything that was repeated in multiple sessions will be simplified to keep this as brief and meaningful as possible.

Explanation of Program:

All the SM's stated that they worked for the Fiverr Customer Relation's team. Most identified themselves as both an Account Manager and a Success Manager, although it seems like in later contacts "account manager" was used less. The SM's stated that the Seller Success program was created to help sellers who seemed to have the greatest potential for continued success on Fiverr. Little mention was made about the level of the seller, but some implied that level 2 sellers in the program might be considered for promotions if they applied the suggestions made. Some of the users who were chatting with their SM's expressed skepticism about the usefulness of the program since they weren't all happy with their current experiences on Fiverr. While all intended to stay with Fiverr and were earning money, some reported to their SM's that they had trouble with PayPal chargebacks, canned responses from Customer Support and Fiverr features that seemed non-functional or didn't result in the advantages that were promised.

The Success Managers themselves responded vaguely to many of the early questions and inquiries. There were some specifics given as follows: The SM's across the board said attempts were being made to add to the number of CS reps and to improve the quality of CS responses. One SM stated that he was aware of problems with PayPal chargebacks and that it was discussed often by staff, but he was unable to give any specific information on how or when Fiverr might work on the issue. One area the SM's did seem concerned about was reports of non-functional or poorly implemented features. They asked questions about the analytics page and what could be changed (far prior to the new analytics changes in 2017) as well as other specific seller pages. They responded to seller concerns about problems with inbox messages. Statements were made regarding attempts to shut down problems with sellers using false profiles to gain access to buyers and then to use the inbox as a way of quickly acquiring off-Fiverr contact info. According to one SM, the users of these fake seller accounts were not concerned about being banned because they only created a gig to get access to Buyer Requests and an available contact button. Once those sellers gained access to a buyer's email or Skype ID, they apparently continued discussions off-Fiverr. For this reason, Fiverr intended to monitor inboxes more closely than before. I suggested that some of the sellers helping gather information might want to ask specific questions about Buyer

Requests and what could be done to tame the spam. I did not receive much feedback on this and the one seller who definitely asked about it did not receive an answer.

GENERAL TIPS BASED ON OVERALL SUCCESS MANAGER GUIDES

Summary/Takeaways:

- **PayPal Chargebacks are still a problem. It is best to continue to report problems with these to Customer Support, in any offered live events with Fiverr staff, and if you do have an SM, bring this up again. Otherwise, these are a fact of business on Fiverr, so everyone should be cautious about large orders from new buyers (break up large orders into multiple small ones) and keep an eye out for red flags.**
- **Feature Issues: Fiverr is making an attempt to address broken features or ones that are not fully functional. The SM's are interested in these, so it will continue to be helpful to report these to CS and other staff.**
- **Inbox Messages: It seems likely that there are some sellers abusing the inbox by using false profiles to gain access to**

buyer information. These false sellers have no concerns about bans since they have no intention of selling. To avoid the chances of your own account being identified as false take these steps:
- Avoid words that make your inbox appear with a red outline. (Words like email, payment.)
- Words that don't result in the red outline can still get you noticed. Using phrases like "outside contact" or "contact me" seem to be some of the more problematic. Try to avoid using these kinds of phrases. If necessary, use the inbox message for basic introductions to your clients and then use attachments to exchange longer pieces of information.

WARNING: **Do NOT use the attachment system to abuse the real rules and offer your contact info or ask buyer's for theirs when it isn't related to a gig order on Fiverr. Do not discuss outside payment in attachments. If sellers begin to abuse attachments it's possible Fiverr will remove the option for attachments outside of the order page.**

It's also possible that they will increase monitoring of attachments which could be detrimental to all sellers. This is especially true for sellers who genuinely need to exchange personal data for gig reasons, like gigs requiring website credentials or email addresses acquired to create business cards.

CHAPTER ONE

Success Manager Tips on Skills and Profile

These are tips that were specifically sent to my source group. The first ones will be related to setting up your Fiverr profile.

- Your profile picture should be an actual photo of you, a caricature of you, or your company logo.

There are some pitfalls to watch out for here. What the SM may not tell you is that there are some good ways to apply this and some poor ways. There are also some things to consider when deciding which of the above to choose. Let's go over some of those.

Deciding on a profile picture:

The most-recommended choice by many Top Rated Sellers, Fiverr Ambassadors, Success Managers, and other successful people is a face shot of yourself, with you smiling and in professional dress. Consider seller Ozzieuk who uses his profile picture as a big part of his brand. If you feel able to get a good photo like that, it can be a ticket to sales. Buyers like to know who they are dealing with, they like a warm welcome, and they appreciate a professional appearance. You may have specific reasons you don't want to use a selfie, even a really good one. Some people just really, really value their privacy or have reasons not to display their real photos on Fiverr. What are some reasons people might not want to?

People who have a complex family or relationship situation may need to keep a lower profile online. People who are recognizable in a photo because they are well known in another field may not want to display a personal photo. People who have small children at home or some other sensitive issue may just not feel comfortable. Forum moderators* like FontHaunt (www.fiverr.com/fonthaunt) have sometimes dealt with issues since forum users may not always be happy about the moderator and not realize that moderators are just sellers who do what they are asked to by staff.

If you still really want to follow the photo advice, there are some things you can do to make it work. You can hire another freelancer or get a talented friend or family member to help you with these if you don't know how to do them on your own. There are methods that can be used to enhance a photo that will make it look great, but not make you as recognizable as you might think. Many, many sellers use these tricks without anyone even realizing exactly what they are doing. Some ways to do these include:

- Taking a photo at an unusual angle which obscures your identity but

still shows a pleasing human appearance
- Editing a photo with artistic effects to make it look like a drawing, painting or illustration which can make it less recognizable
- Editing a photo with special effects to blur, smooth, or fade a photo so that it no longer looks exactly like other photos of you
- Using a photo of yourself with a very different hairstyle, sunglasses or glasses, a hat, or clothing items
- Using a photo of someone else - this one should really be a very last choice and shouldn't be used in most situations. If you use a photo that is just a plain stock photo you may violate copyright and it can make you appear dishonest when people find your picture in a simple reverse search. If you have access to a photo of someone who isn't known and doesn't appear elsewhere online, you need to have the permission of that person to use the photo.

In rare cases, this might be helpful since you may have a relative who never plans to be online and takes a great picture and doesn't mind being on your "team" as the "face" of your account. Just remember that this can come back to haunt you since people change their minds. If you build a great successful brand and that face becomes iconic, the person could change their mind, and no matter how sure you are that they won't, you would have trouble legally if they insist on the removal of their photo. They might decide they don't want the recognition, they may decide to go online after all, and they may even decide to capitalize on your success by branching out into their own business venture. Be careful with this one and use another option if possible!

Many sellers do use a caricature or avatar of themselves as a profile photo. This may have mixed results. If you are already a graphic designer or you sell artistic gigs, this can be a chance for you to showcase your skills. The thing is, it is not that hard to create a "cartoonized" version of a photo of yourself, but to get one that actually looks appealing is not so easy. Buyers don't want to see a simplistic pop art character that could be anyone, because that is no better than using a stock photo of some blonde girl with a headset as a "genuine" photo. To really capitalize on a caricature, it should be something extra special. Perhaps you do have a great talent at making a simple cartoon of a photo look especially realistic or to take on a style that is unique and amazing. There is a Fiverr seller named Zeus777 (www.fiverr.com/zeus777) who does incredible anime and other cartoon styles and I can recognize her images as her work in many cases. By using her own work as her profile photo, she actually enhances her profile with a caricature/avatar.

The last recommended option is to use a logo as your profile photo. There are reasons to do this and reasons not to. For example, it's fairly easy to grab a cool looking logo from Google images and it may look amazing when you pop it into your Fiverr profile. Perhaps you even take out whatever text is on it or use one without text and add your username/brand to make it your own. It might look great. If you aren't a graphic designer or logo designer, this might work. Even then, it isn't recommended. Just like using a stock photo, a logo like that can be found easily and give you the appearance of dishonesty even when you didn't intend to do anything dishonest.

You can also use online or offline software to create a logo. This has a similar effect and can look really good if you aren't a designer yourself. It has the same problem, though, since software often uses well-known templates. In both cases, you also risk violating copyright and getting banned on Fiverr for doing so. There are also many sellers on Fiverr who have heard that logo design is a hot field, easy, and they want to get started doing that. They pick up some free or pirated logo-creation software and they make an account. The first logo they make is their own. This will really tank your success somewhere down the road, and it's even worse if it happens after you have 10, 50, 100 or more reviews. Buyers are becoming savvier about logos and they are also becoming more jaded. Many buyers spend $5-50 on a cheap logo on Fiverr and are shocked when they get something of poor quality or taken from elsewhere. No matter how you try to spin it, taking art from someone else is stealing. If you claim to be a logo designer, you need to really learn how to use software to draw vector images and use your artistic skills to make your very own designs. That includes the design for your own logo. If you don't know what a vector image is, you are already in trouble as a designer.

So, if you aren't a graphic designer yourself but you do want to use a logo, you still want one that is original and high quality. It may sound like this is the easiest route to go, and for some people it is. You'll just have to try and weigh the results for yourself. You can make a stab at creating your own logo if you really do think you have the skills. Put it on your profile and see how it goes. Your Success Manager probably wouldn't recommend this, but if you don't have one of your own to ask, it's really up to you. A better choice might be to hire someone to create a logo for you. There are thousands of mediocre to poor logo designers on Fiverr and dozens of really good ones. If you don't have a lot to spend, consider just getting something very simple. A signature logo with your username on it will be unique since no one has your username but you. If you can afford something better and you want to invest in it, you might look at some of the Top Rated Seller who does logo design and try it out. Twistedweb123 is a well-known Fiverr Ambassador who sells logos, though they might not be for everyone. Take a look at the samples for him or for other designers and do reverse searches to make sure what they are selling looks original. Show some samples to your friends and family. If you know other sellers on Fiverr, ask for their opinions on samples or on a referral for a logo designer. Whatever you do, just make sure that if you use a logo, use the best quality you possibly can and make SURE you are the only one using it.

Summary/Takeaways:

Fiverr prefers that you use a picture of yourself as your profile picture, but they are open to a caricature or original logo.

If you worry about using a recognizable photo of yourself, consider using a good photo of yourself at an unusual angle or artistically rendered so that it still represents YOU but can't be easily found in reverse searches. If you don't even want to be recommended on the street, this can still be done!

When choosing to use a logo, be sure that yours is branded with your business name or username (often the same thing) and that it is 100% unique. Using even a bit of clipart can really put you in a bad place if someone accuses you of dishonesty or copyright violation.

WARNING: Do not try to use an easy-to-find stock photo and pretend that it's your picture. Rookie mistake. Don't use copyrighted photos or art as this is a Terms of Service violation and can get you in serious trouble on Fiverr.

*There are usernames for various real Fiverr users listed throughout this book. As long as the user is mentioned in a positive way, the username is given as it is at the time of this writing. If the author uses a negative example, the username will be altered to a fictional name to avoid putting any real seller in a negative light. There is no way to be sure that all of the sellers mentioned will keep the same account or gigs over time. You can go to fiverr.com/username to find any seller who still has an active account.

CHAPTER TWO

Specifics on Profile

When you fill out the rest of your profile, the Success Manager advice that has been given to many is this:

- Make sure that your user profile is complete including languages, skills, linked accounts, and education
- Your profile should include your experience and explain why the buyer should choose YOU
- Your location should be accurate and not displaying a different country than where you live
- Your Gigs should offer different services and not copies of the same service
- Use your real name

These are general tips but very important. Do you have to follow them to a **T**? It really depends on what you want to do, but if you had a Success Manager they would say yes. Still, there are pros and cons to evaluate and then you can decide what to do.

Filling out your profile with your language, skills, linked accounts, and education is fairly important. You also want to use genuine information and don't just fill in what you think will look good. It isn't necessary to have a specific degree or certificate to be successful. If you DO want something to look good, there are ways to acquire things you can display without a lot of time or finances.

Language is particularly important in some categories. If you are a translator, writer, or seller of business services, it really matters to list your languages thoroughly and accurately. For example, if you have a gig offering a translation of English to Spanish, you need to state that you speak both English and Spanish and list whether or not you are fluent. A buyer MIGHT still use you even if you aren't fluent, so don't put it down just because you need cash. Some buyers will pay a premium to get a translation from someone who is a native Spanish speaker but lives in an English speaking place (or the opposite.)

Other buyers need a bargain. If you put down that you had 2 years of high school Spanish and read it well but live in the United States, they might want to buy from you. You may be able to charge a little less, use a software translator to help and still produce a decent translation. If you try to fake a buyer out, though, it's going to bite you back eventually. Lots of sellers try to say they can translate ANY language and they even list as many languages as they can on their profiles and put fluent on all of them. Then they try to produce a translation, article or business plan by just a quick copy/paste in Google translate. Some even get some good reviews for a while.

Your skills are also important, and you can play around with this to a certain degree, but only so far. If you list that you are an expert in SEO and that you can guarantee 100% genuine traffic to a website, you may get some sales based on your claim. If the truth is that you can do exactly what you claim, but it's your brother who is an expert and he's right there to help you, then just incorporate him into your "team" and claim it. Only do this if you can actually produce what you claim! If you claim this same expertise and you buy some bot-traffic software from a guy you know and try to send 1 million hits from a random country to your client's U.K. based tobacco shop, you could cause her website to be dropped from Google search. That buyer is going to demand a refund, report you to Customer Support, complain on the forum, and possibly get your account suspended. You can damage a client in a way that impacts their bottom line by doing that. In general, list your skills as they really are.

Your linked accounts should be listed, but how important are they? Fiverr gives you the chance to list your social media accounts and the idea is that if you link them, it makes you look "verified" since you have proven that you own multiple social media accounts. Honesty, in the personal opinion of this author, that's a false assurance to a buyer. What does it really prove if you verify your Facebook, Twitter, etc.? However, Fiverr seems to think that it does help and some sellers swear by it. There really is no harm in doing it and the Success Manager would want to you check that box, so you might as well do it.

Your education can be important, but there are ways to make that shine without lying about it if you don't have much to list that is special. If you really do have university degrees, especially ones relevant to what you do, by all means, do list them. If you don't have them, don't list them. It's tempting to make one up, but if you were to skyrocket to success it could be another "come back to haunt you" issue. There are Fiverr sellers who have gone from nothing to earnings in excess of a million US dollars annually, sometimes within their first year on Fiverr. No, it's not common, but with Success Managers around it could become more common.

If you give in to temptation while you are level 1 or 2 and you list a degree from a solid school, it's very easy to check that later. If you didn't even attend that school, or perhaps were there for a month in 1999, just don't try and put down a degree. Don't forget that you DO want to list other useful bits of info. Did you join an honor society in high school or college? List it if you can. Did you earn a certificate for being firefighter of the month when you volunteered and you sell e-books on fire safety? Put that certificate down! See the next section on Skills for more ideas regarding Skills Tests, Fiverr Learn and more.

Success Managers have comments about gig types. Your gigs should be different and there are ways to capitalize on similar gigs in a way that won't get you in trouble, or you can just stick with entirely different gigs. Many sellers (and some success managers) say that it's best to focus on one skill area and not be a jack of all trades. I think that depends on the seller, but since branding is a party of owning a business, there might be some truth to that. If you do want to expand your gigs and are trying to find ways to list gigs in the same or similar categories without duplicating, take a look at how some other level 2 and Top Rated Sellers do it. Look at voiceover artist annai80 (www.fiverr.com/annai80.) She has multiple gigs in her category, but they aren't just the same gig with different pictures or a gig with a word or two different and the same pictures. I've seen sellers who try this and it's awful. Instead, Annai80 took the time to consider different types of services in the category that might draw in a buyer who is looking to narrow their approach. It works and can "cast a bigger net." The sellers who try to put up 5 gigs that are the same exact thing in different categories can get banned and it just doesn't look professional.

Success Managers have also commented about seller names. The name issue is an interesting one. Success Managers recommend the use of a real name, and I would have to assume this means putting your real name in your profile and other places since usernames are often more reflective of the service. (Some people do put their names as their usernames, but many don't.) I think that the reason they suggest using your real name is that calling yourself "Logoartist57574" doesn't sound personal at all and buyers may feel less comfortable. Worst yet, some sellers go by silly names like "poohbysnugs68" and that doesn't tell people anything about you, at least not anything positive. You are more likely to be successful if buyers see you as a real person. So, it's probably not what name you use as much as it is that you use a name and not an impersonal tag. I know many sellers who use a pseudonym, nickname or short version of their name. I use my middle name for many things and my nickname for others, but even in "real life" no one calls me by my first name and most people don't even know it. So, I can't be sure what your own Success Manager would tell you, but I think the name issue is about seeming human.

Summary/Takeaways:

- Do list languages that you can read/write/speak. Don't try to list a fluency level that is inaccurate. Don't claim that you speak anything "native" unless you really do.
- List your skills for SURE but list your real level of expertise in those!
- Link your accounts because Fiverr seems to find it important and maybe some buyers do too. In the opinion of this author, it's not that important as long as you have one or two.
- Education IS important but don't fall for the temptation to fake it. Put down what is true and can be verified by the school.
- Offer multiple gigs if you can, but don't offer the same exact service with multiple titles.
- List a first name or nickname somewhere, or at least sign your messages in a personal way. While you don't want to be so personal that you call a buyer "buddy" or "bro" you do want to seem like a human being.

WARNING: Be honest about your location. Yes, you can get away with faking it, maybe even for a long time. Some people use a VPN or even more sophisticated means to hide their location and it can work. Most of them don't know how to do it well enough to not get caught. Even if you think you do, Fiverr implements new things (like the current phone verification) that can trip you up.

No matter how good you are at it, if you want to succeed like you had a Success Manager, don't risk it. I guarantee you there are real sellers making very good money in the USA, Nigeria, the U.K., Pakistan, Australia, India, and anywhere else. Don't let anyone tell you it can't be done. If you fake it and THEN you succeed, what are you going to do when Forbes Magazine calls YOU to be in an article? Forbes interviewed several Fiverr sellers in a previous article. If you are caught lying, it's over.

CHAPTER THREE

A More Polished Profile

If you don't have any special certificates or degrees for skills and you want to, check out online schools like Kaplan and Western Governors. You don't have to invest tens of thousands for a poor degree that you aren't going to use, so even though those are offered, don't sign up for one unless you have a good reason. On the other hand, you might find a three-month course in graphic design with a certificate of completion and it might cost only a few hundred dollars. That might be worth it, especially if you'll really learn something. If that is still out of your budget or you don't sell anything related, look at courses on sites like Udemy or even Warrior Forum. Some of those are NOT worth the money, so be cautious, but you can find something that might be useful on sites like that. Udemy has courses in many things that freelancers do. A lot of those come with a certificate of completion for only $5-25. If you want some "resume padding" that is still real, consider that.

As of late 2018, Fiverr also has a new option called Fiverr Learn. You can take courses offered by successful sellers who have already done well as freelancers. Some of the course materials are offered for less elsewhere, but not all of them. Even so, there may be advantages in using Fiverr Learn. Early feedback has indicated that the courses themselves are pretty good. In addition, if you take a course on Udemy you have no solid proof for Fiverr. If you take a course on Fiverr itself, you can prove it. It can show up right on your profile IF you want it to which gives you extra credibility.

Another slightly newer feature is Skill Endorsement. Your buyers can click on skills that you've demonstrated and that can help you. For this reason, don't just toss any gig up to see if it makes money. Put up gigs for things that you can really do.

Fiverr also began to offer skill tests in 2018. These can be very useful. You can take them repeatedly until you get a reasonably good score. If you get a score that is passing but not high enough to display, your profile will still show a green checkmark on that skill to show that you passed the test. This can be very impressive to buyers who've been burned. Just don't have a friend take a test for you or cheat your way through on Google because you may end up with negative reviews when buyers realize they've been tricked.

The Success Manager Checklist, Titles

Success Managers have overwhelmingly suggested a checklist of tips to help you define your profile, gigs, branding, persona, and SEO. We'll focus on those areas now. At the bottom of each section, I will put the actual checklists that were sent to some of my seller friends or a list of suggested takeaways based on the SM advice.

The title of your gig should be clear, should accurately describe your service, but shouldn't be so long that it can't be quickly absorbed. Prior to early 2017, titles were a very tricky issue. The problem was that Fiverr search definitely utilized the keywords in the title as an important part of the search process. For a while, people had to really manipulate titles in some quirky ways to get that to work. For example, if you had a title that said: "I will remove a back ground from your picture" that might describe your service well, but it could make you really lose out in a search process. Since most people write background but some do write back ground, you would only cover the words back and ground but not background. Besides that, many people might search "Photoshop background" and they wouldn't find you at all. This led to lots of titles on Fiverr that looked odd. You would see "I will do background back ground remove removal Photoshop" as a title, and that isn't a title at all. Technically, though, it covers more keywords.

As of this writing, the search still does lean more toward titles than it really should, but the Success Managers have said that Fiverr is trying to change that. They are really working on the search tag aspect under your gig edit section and eventually search should utilize that more. So, their suggestion is to work on titles that read like titles and have proper grammar and spelling, etc.

So, the first items on your checklist should be:

- **Is your gig title clear?**
- **Does your gig title accurately describe your service?**
- **Is your title within the recommended length? (When you type the title in on Fiverr, it will warn you when it gets too long.)**
- **Does your title still have some appropriate keywords in it?**
- **Does your title use proper grammar?**
- **Is everything spelled correctly?**

CHAPTER FOUR

The Success Manager Checklist, Services

The Success Manager checklists have also gone into some depth about the services you offer. There is some indication that Fiverr really wants to emphasize professionalism as we approach later 2017 and 2018. They also seem to recommend that you work on your branding as much as you can, so that means that you have to turn your business into more than just a little freelance pocket change to succeed on Fiverr in the way SM's want you to! Let's get into what they recommend.

When you create a single gig, the SM's recommend that it offer a single service. Don't try to cram too much into one gig. Here's an example:

Seller guitardednes1 offers a writing gig. In one gig, he offers to write articles about anything, newspaper articles, investigative reports, resumes, letters, business books, horror novels, and poetry. That is WAY too much to focus on. Sure, it might lead to people ordering because they are excited about one-stop shopping and that's great. But it can also lead to people missing all those details and not finding him at all, or negative reviews when the gig is misunderstood.

Seller fonthaunt offers one gig to do blog writing and it even hones in on a niche for pet-related articles. There is another gig to create animal-related promo videos. Another gig focuses even tighter and offers website content about horses. This can spin off into other areas as well. These are not exactly the same and they may not even use the same tools, but it's a way of offering one TYPE of service but multiple subcategories for that.

Success Managers have also hinted that they like accounts with a strong focus on just one category, and that may be good advice if you are getting a high volume of sales in that category. My friends who are more successful than I am with freelancing (with and without Success Managers) don't always see it that way. Some really believe it at least branching out in a few related categories. I don't think it hurts, especially if you can tie them together under your brand. After all, Kellogg's sells a lot more than cereal, but as consumers, we do associate the brand with food products overall. It's really up to the individual seller.

Trying to sell a huge number of gigs in wildly different categories may not be the best idea while you are building your brand, though. Once you are making a ton of money and maybe you even have a TRS badge, no one may care if you have 25 gigs that relate to your brand and 5 wild cards. If you aren't there yet, the SM checklist recommends sticking close to a category or a set of related categories and subcategories.

Categories, Subcategories, Service Types

Success Managers also offer advice on categories, subcategories and service types. Not all categories have subcategories and not all gigs have service types, so if those don't relate to what you do, don't worry about it. What seems to matter most is accuracy. Your gig will probably fit in more than one category unless you sell something really niche or narrow. For example, if you sell mascot logo design, that doesn't give you a lot of room to move around, so you would want to choose the exact category for what you sell. If you are a graphic designer and you have a gig that offers fliers, posters and virtual fliers, you might be able to fit that into more than one potential category.

The biggest mistake you can make here is to put a gig in an inaccurate category to try to manipulate something in the system. That can really get you in trouble and it sure won't be recommended by a Success Manager.

I saw a seller recently, I won't give the name here since this is entirely negative, but he was advising other sellers to try his new idea. He made a gig for logo design and he only found 3 recent buyer requests that matched his gig. He applied for those three. Then he paused the gig which allowed him to change his category to Photoshop Editing. He went to Buyer Requests and applied for 2 more offers there, offering his logo design (in Photoshop) to those buyers. Then he changed to the Programming and Tech category and send his offer to two buyers who were IT business users, and he offered to make them logos. At that point he was spamming, no question about it. Besides that, if Fiverr had reviewed his gig at that moment and found him listing logo design in Programming and Tech, they probably would have permanently denied his gig. If he had a few reviews, they would have been lost. Bam! Don't do it. Fiverr already prevents major category changes on active gigs but allows them on paused gigs. They may shut that option down later, but it's not a good idea even though you can do it.

Put your gig in the best and most accurate category for what you sell and try to leave it there. If you feel like you need to be in another, consider creating a related gig that isn't exactly the same and try that gig in the other category as long as it's an accurate fit. This isn't to say you can't tweak your gigs and try other categories if they are reasonably accurate and that does happen. I've changed a gig from a general writing focus to a niche writing focus, but the reviews still applied to my service. Just try to find the best spot and leave it for a while, and don't choose an unrelated category or leave a gig in a category where it isn't working just to be different.

So, for this chapter, here is your checklist:

- Do you have the services you sell narrowed to specific themes and established in one gig per service?
- If you offer multiple services, do you have each service in its own gig?
- Are you trying to offer too many services in very distant categories instead of building your brand?
- Is your gig in the most accurate category?
- If you are already getting some results in your category, do you need to refine

or tweak your subcategory or service types?

CHAPTER FIVE

Success Manager Tips: Gig Descriptions

When it comes to gig descriptions, our Success Manager polls show that the Success Management program has specific suggestions for descriptions but they are easy to follow. No need to get too worried about the description except for the number one rule. That number one rule is that your description MUST clearly explain to the buyer what they will get if they buy any of your gig packages. This really cannot be overemphasized. When you spell out what your gig sells, what is covered in packages and what is NOT covered by a purchase, you will make your life easier. The majority of complaints that end up at Fiverr Customer Support door are (reportedly) about communication issues that started when the buyer didn't read or didn't understand the gig description. That doesn't mean the fault is all on the buyer, though, far from it. It really means the opposite.

If your writing isn't getting across a precision description and the buyer just clicks order, the chances of ending up with a dispute, revision request, cancellation or bad review are increased tenfold. It isn't easy to write a good description when you create a new gig and that's totally understandable, so here are some recommendations for how to start and then how to refine one:

When you write your gig description, read it and re-read it before you even publish the gig. Once you think it's pretty good, wait overnight. Read it again and see if you find anything unclear, explained poorly, or left out. Remember that your buyers will be reading in English but their reading comprehension will vary a lot. Try to use clear English that isn't condescending but is fairly simple. Avoid complicated terms unless you can define them. If they must be there for your gig type, make FAQ's for your gig to help explain them.

Once you are that far, read your description again. Think you have it? Don't publish yet. Next get a friend or family member (preferably who is fluent in English) to read your description and tell you what they think they would be getting if they ordered. Have them try to mess things up by telling you what could go wrong. Once you have it refined a bit more, have a few more people read it. This time try to get some to read who are fluent and skilled in English as well as some who don't read English well. Middle-school kids and teenagers make great critics who can tell you if you are patronizing or writing at too high a level. When you refine it this time, publish the gig (assuming all else is done.) At first, keep a lenient policy for revisions and be willing to work a lot to make a buyer happy.

Take special note of what causes buyers to submit revision requests or to ask a lot of questions. This can help you re-write your description again. Your gig will drop in and out of search while you edit, so just deal with it, it's part of the process and it's worth it. Once you are getting some deliveries done with fewer questions and few or no revision requests, you can probably let things ride for a while and get a bit tougher about giving away free revisions or canceling. If you do run into trouble, take notes but don't keep revising like crazy if you are getting some orders. Wait it out for a few weeks and then you might want to tweak it again. If you aren't getting any sales, check to see if you've made your gig too complicated to understand or so simplistic that it doesn't sound like a good value. You WILL get there.

No matter what category you are in, your grammar, spelling and punctuation do matter. Some matter more than others, but in general, you need to have a basic command of English and the ability to convey concepts and communication with buyers. If your gigs are not directly related to writing, editing, proofreading, translating, English transcription, resume services or other highly language-specific tasks, you can probably manage with just that basic ability except that you'll want the buyer to see you as a pro from the first read-through. You don't have to be great at writing in English to make that happen. If you are a great illustrator or an SEO guru you can get by with just good communication skills but the first time a buyer reads your profile and description, there should be no obvious spelling errors, typos or major grammar/punctuation errors. What do I mean by obvious and major? Check this out:

User desingprotect44 has this in the gig description:
"I cna make a logo that you will die. When you see my ecksellent desings u can be so happy."
This fails to meet the criteria set out by Success Managers even if the description is longer.

Summary/Takeaways:

- **Make sure that your gig description clearly states what is included (or not) in the service.**
- **Make sure that the gig description has correct grammar, spelling, and punctuation**
- **Highlights and bolds should be used sparingly and only where appropriate**

WARNING: There are pitfalls to avoid in this area. If your English is poor or you speak and read fluently but don't use grammar well, you can have a friend help. You can also hire a proofreader. There are people who will write your entire gig description for you. If you offer a technical service it may not be a bad idea to get someone to write your description for you.

You will still need to be able to communicate with buyers in reasonably good English, so when you message with buyers use a spell checker and a service like Grammarly. DOUBLE CHECK! When the name "Fiverr" is written all over the site, it looks extremely unprofessional and sloppy if you write "Fiber" or even "5er" when your English isn't excellent. The PITFALL is that if you want to offer a service that involves writing (article writing, resume writing, translation) and you have someone else write your gig description, your buyer may think that the writing in the description shows YOUR abilities. If they order based on that and you write with typos or grammar problems you will either end up with bad reviews or you will get banned for fraud.

CHAPTER SIX

Success Manager Tips: Advanced Gig Descriptions

The SM's have been clear with users about minimal points with Gig Extras but we'll cover those here.

First and foremost, Success Managers recommend that sellers do use gig extras when possible. These are excellent for upselling. Even a brand new seller who has to price gigs very low (even $5-10 for a basic package) can really make more money by creatively using Gig Extras. Let's use a highly recommended Top Rated Seller as an example, however. Voiceover seller sue_mcl (fiverr.com/sue_mcl) has one gig that is low cost. She offers a 3 minute pre-recorded item for a very reasonable price. One might think that she isn't going to make as much from that gig since it costs less than others. Once you click on the gig, though, she offers a gig extra that upgrades your delivery substantially for more. The price isn't so high as to put buyers off, but it is attractive, so more buyers are likely to go ahead and add the extra. Since she did this with a gig that has pre-recorded content, the extra will only take her a bit of added time. Both the buyer and the seller have something big to gain.

SM's recommend that the extras be unique and clear. This voiceover artist does this well. The extra is defined with simple words and offers something that is unique since it isn't already offered in the main gig. This is an excellent method for following Success Manager advice and it really helps make gigs more successful and earns more money for the seller and Fiverr. Buyers also get the chance to see that they may need something they hadn't thought of and they will purchase the extra.

Sometimes there are services that Fiverr offers as built-in extras. In the voiceover category we've been talking about, the Commercial License was one of these as of 2018. (This may have changed, but for example purposes, we will assume that the Commercial License is a built-in on these gigs.) Success Managers do not want sellers to duplicate the built-in extras and offer them a second time as a self-created extra. This goes against SM recommendations and could cause a problem with Fiverr Trust and Safety.

Summary/Takeaways:

- **Make sure that your extras are clearly defined and unique**
- **Don't duplicate built-in extras**

WARNING: Be careful not to trick buyers into using extras that they don't need. I've seen sellers who offer something as part of the package and then sell it as an extra as well. For example, a seller might have a brief mention in a logo gig stating that they include a source file free with every order. As a buyer, if I see that I can buy the source file (perhaps a vector or PSD) for $10 as an extra, I might not realize it was already supposed to be included. If I pay for that and realize it later, I can complain to Customer Support. This is unethical for sellers to do at least and at worst it could get the seller's gig removed or the account banned.

CHAPTER SEVEN

Success Manager Tips- Marketing

When it comes to how a gig looks, Success Managers understand the same thing that marketing professionals teach. You have only a moment to get a buyer's attention and perhaps another moment to hold it. You want a buyer to stick around and read enough of your gig title and description to know if the gig might be what they need. As a buyer myself, I don't even always realize I want to buy a gig until I see a really eye-catching gig image and click out of curiosity. It might not even be a gig I was interested in or knew about. Once intrigued I'm likely to add least add the gig to my favorites for later. It's not that unusual for me to worry that I'll forget and to go ahead and order the gig right then. There is a seller at www.fiverr.com/dynamitedork that I have favorited now. I just came across his gig while looking for stock photos of cowboys. Dynamitedork offers videos of himself doing a cowboy impression and I decided I was going to find a reason to buy it! His video thumbnail helped get my attention.

Success Managers recommend that you spend some significant time on your 3 primary gig images and really make them unique and eye-catching. If you need help with that, you can hire someone or you can just do some tutorials in Photoshop or even an online image editor. You can do some amazing things with just a little polish. Do some research on what colors are used by marketing professionals and why. What does red do? Does it grab attention, make people feel angry or make them excited? Does green make people happy because it's the color of many types of money? Does grey make people want to click away? There are excellent free sites about marketing and both free and paid e-books that cover these things. See what you can find!

Utilize the same techniques in your gig video. It isn't absolutely necessary to have a gig video for some services, but SM's recommend it. Since it's a tool available to all sellers, why not? If you don't know how to create a video or think you need expensive software, which is resolvable. You can hire someone to make a video for you if you want to. You can make a video using free software by just searching the web for ideas. All you need is a simple slideshow saved as an mp4. If you want to do a video showing you talking to your clients it can be very effective. You can do this with a phone camera if you have a bit of knowledge of lighting and video editing. There are tons of YouTube tutorials to teach you how to make a smartphone video better. If you plan to make many action videos you can invest in a used GoPro and a Blue Yeti microphone without breaking the bank. It isn't absolutely necessary to have these tools, though, it's just something to consider.

Summary/Takeaways:

- **Create an eye-catching gig image**
- **If possible, use a gig video and have an eye-catching video thumbnail**

- **Utilize ALL of your image gallery - have at least three gig images and possibly PDF files/portfolio as well**

CHAPTER EIGHT

Success Manager Advanced Tips - Marketing and Price

Success Managers recommend that you make sure your prices are appropriate, but what does that really mean? In the old days on Fiverr, all gigs were $5 and you could only upsell with extras if they were even available. Later on, you could sell at higher prices but you had to have something available at $5. Things have really changed since 2015. As of 2019, you can price pretty much however you wish unless you have a Fiverr Pro badge. If you do have a Fiverr Pro badge, the gigs that are marked as "Pro" must start at $100. As of this writing, Pros can have gigs that start at lower prices, but those gigs cannot have a Pro badge. Of course, this is not all good for those who get the Pro badge. They are held to a high standard by Fiverr and their buyers. If a client is unhappy with a $25 gig, they might just go away without leaving a review. If a client spent $150 to purchase one gig and they don't love it, they may be really upset. How do YOU decide if your pricing is appropriate?

Another thing to know about the earlier Fiverr origins is that most sellers had to start selling at $5 and they were told to over-deliver every time. These cheap prices and over-delivery mindset was probably tough on sellers since they may have worked many hours to earn $4 after commission. There were no processing fees for buyers, so a buyer could get an amazing deal for $5-10.

Even though this was probably very hard on those sellers at first, quite a few of them are still selling on Fiverr today. Why? Several of them went on to be featured on television news and in magazine articles. Some did burn the midnight oil and work very hard, but they sold thousands of gigs in a very short time. They learned how to work as quickly as possible while still producing good quality. They learned to make their services smaller (micro-jobs) and put in a more reasonable amount of work over time.

At the time, Fiverr recommended that sellers work toward services that only took 5-15 minutes to accomplish. There were no Success Managers but the CEO of Fiverr was vocal about his dream. The sellers who were able to get the timing right could make $4 every 5-10 minutes. That could add up to $48 in an hour. Many of those sellers worked 12 hours a day including weekends to get their businesses started. They could make $4000 in a week at that time. Reporters who interviewed Fiverr and their early Top Rated Sellers said that a hard-working seller could bank over $150,000 a year even with some off time during summer and holidays. Those sellers probably didn't want to keep up that pace forever (not counting a few workaholics) but some of them now have over 25,000 positive reviews. Today they can sell at prices that aren't that much higher, perhaps $25-50 per well-delivered gig. Some have topped one million dollars in sales in a year.

We can learn a lot from those early sellers. For new sellers or those who have hit a slump, approaching Fiverr like the original sellers can make sense temporarily. A new seller might want to sell at $5-10 and do hours of work to get one good review for a $4 profit. Once they have 100 reviews they can scale up! It's an investment of time but doesn't cost anything otherwise. A seller who has been selling at higher prices but is in a downturn can lower prices temporarily and do the same thing. There is still room to utilize low-cost gigs with excellent deliveries just to get over a hump.

Today it isn't uncommon to see a new seller posting on the forum with a complaint that other sellers are selling too much for $5. Others complain that they have 5 good reviews but can't get new orders with their gigs priced at $50. They aren't always wrong about part of the point. It's hard to compete with sellers who will do a day's work for $5. It's hard to feel satisfied if you have a degree in web development but you can't sell a website for $50 when off-Fiverr developers can make $300. The complainers don't always think about the reason to stop complaining and start working hard to get where they want to be.

One new seller might gain the most benefit by competing with $5 sellers and offer the same service for $5-15 but have better gig images, a better description and deliver a better service. They will gain repeat customers and tons of good reviews. Later they can raise prices and still beat the $5 sellers even while charging much more. Another seller may choose to sell at a slightly higher price even while new, but demonstrate something so impressive that clients pay attention.

A client who sees one seller with a logo gig at $5 and another seller with a logo gig at $50 may stop to look a bit closer. If the $50 seller has beautiful logo samples, 8 good reviews that appear to be real, original logos that weren't stolen from somewhere else - that seller suddenly looks promising. The $5 seller might have one or more of those factors but not all of them. They might have good reviews but poor or copied samples. They might have good samples but they may not be able to communicate well enough to understand the buyer's needs in an English language conversation.

Whatever you decide to do, your prices may have to shift up and down some to get more sales during slow periods and capitalise on trends. Some sellers find that higher prices help eliminate "bargain hunter" buyers and it's worth losing some sales as those clients may be very demanding. Some sellers may find that higher prices attract buyers who are more professional. Other sellers really prefer to work cheap and fast and make money the way the old-fashioned sellers did.

It is true that Success Managers push sellers to drive their prices up as much as they can, given the supply and demand issues. Fiverr makes more money when sellers make more money, so that makes sense. If you do price low, you probably have the best chance of eventually attaining a TRS or Pro badge if you can command higher prices at some point.

Summary/Takeaways:

- **Consider Pricing - Too High, Too Low or Just Right?**
- **Take note of the pros and cons with your pricing**

Success Manager Tips- Packages

If your category allows for packages, Success Managers strongly recommend that you use the triple-package feature. Most categories do allow this and it can be a great way to scale your prices. The packages are typically classified as Basic, Standard, and Premium. An average seller who at least has a level 1 badge will probably want at least a $10 base package (perhaps $5 if the market is slow) and then scaled up prices for the other two packages. Fiverr tries to display the Standard package most prominently, so generally speaking you want to try for a simple setup:

Make your Basic Package inexpensive and worth something, but don't offer a lot in the Basic package. This package can be a great way to offer a short consultation or a sample work. You want buyers to find a reason to check out that package and maybe buy it, but overall you want to pull them toward the Standard (middle) Package. The Standard package is usually your average offering that gives good value at a moderate price and is worth it to you as a seller but also available to a buyer on a moderate budget. It doesn't have to cater to low budget buyers. The Premium package should offer all the bells and whistles. This package will be great for buyers with deeper pockets who really want the best money can buy. You may not sell as many Premium packages (depending on your category) but you'll sell some of your gigs are well written.

When it comes to the writing on your package titles and descriptions, makes sure they are very clear. Use your larger gig description to elaborate and explain but make sure that it doesn't contradict anything in your package descriptions. You can use extras to offer even more or to allow for gradual upgrades. Your FAQs can cover whatever clients might ask and whatever won't fit elsewhere.

Summary/Takeaways:

- **Activate the Triple Package Feature if you can**
- **Make sure your Package Descriptions match what you will really deliver**

CHAPTER NINE

FAQs and More

The FAQ feature was a great addition to Fiverr's offerings. It wasn't available for sellers who started out on Fiverr in its early stages. Buyers often don't want to read a very long description but they will skim the Questions in your FAQ section. If something catches their attention they will click to read the answer. You can provide an enormous amount of info in the FAQ section and avoid cancellations or misunderstandings.

Success Managers have said that there are many reasons to use Frequently Asked Questions:

What is the FAQ section good for?

- A chance to speak more about yourself and your passion
- A chance to sell your services and point out why you should be picked beyond the standard gig description
- A chance to let your customers know your do's and don'ts
- A chance to set real expectations
- More opportunity to explain your pricing structure

Summary/Takeaways:

- **Make sure the FAQ Section is Completed**
- **Go through the bullet points above and use the FAQ to cover those areas**

Use the Live Portfolio if at all possible. SM's strongly encourage it. Some sellers think that LP is only for graphic designers since the LP usually shows an image, but this isn't so. A friend of mine with amazing web development skills (www.fiverr.com/wp_kid) was the first to mention this idea to me. You can utilize it to show buyers a great deal about what you do and how happy your customers are. If you sell something that doesn't involve images such as voiceover, translation or writing - you can still have an excellent Live Portfolio. (You'll find the option to turn on LP in the Gigs section of your Selling features.)

The easiest way to use LP for non-image categories is to create a beautiful image that you will deliver as a "cover" to all your deliver materials. If you will be sending an SEO report, you can create a colorful and attractive image that you will deliver as well. Use your imagination! As an example, though, you could do something like this:

Create an image with the same sizing as a gig image. Use attractive colors and if colors are related to what you sell (I.e. green for investment advice) you can go that direction. Don't put anything too revealing on the image. Clients want to keep their info private in many cases. You can put some generic text, however, and it still looks really good. For example, you might deliver this image:

This image will show up in your Live Portfolio. This particular image may or may not fit your style (and you would want to use your own profile photo if you use one, not a stock photo) but something like this can really dress up your Live Portfolio and make you look great to the Fiverr Editors and to prospective buyers.

CHAPTER TEN

Deliveries

It's very important that your delivery times are accurate, match your actual delivery time and don't break the Terms of Service. Sellers make mistakes with this more often than you might think. For example, if you sell a service promoting a viral video, you might be tempted to offer six months of promotion. Fiverr will only allow your delivery time at a maximum of 30 days. A seller might set the delivery time at 29 days and show proof of the ongoing work with delivery with plans to continuing the promotion up to six months. Fiverr does not allow this. Service promises cannot exceed the delivery time since the delivery would not be complete this way.

Another seller might offer the same service but offer 30 days of promotion. I've seen those who think it is fine to have 1 or 2 day delivery and send proof that they started the promotion. In reality, this is called a partial delivery and it violates the Terms of Service. An empty or partial delivery can get you banned from Fiverr. Don't do it!

Make sure that whatever delivery time you put down is really feasible for you. It's even good to overestimate a bit. If you think you can do a 2000 word translation in 1 day, you might want to make your delivery time 3 days. If the job is harder than you thought or a family emergency comes along, you'll have room to work with. Success Managers recommend that you deliver on time more than 95% of the time and in reality, it should be even better. Late deliveries hurt your search ranking, they are off-putting to buyers, they can result in negative reviews and they don't look good to Editors who are considering you for promotions.

Summary/Takeaways:

- **Make sure the delivery time is reasonable and represents the true time it takes to complete a project**
- **Keep your Delivered on Time rate**

as high as possible and never drop below 95%

You'll want to avoid cancellations whenever possible. Success Managers will tell you that cancellations are really a problem for sellers so you will want to take cancellation-avoidance steps from gig creation to order handling. The cancellation issue is major for both buyers and sellers, especially after changes made in 2018.

Buyers have come to think of Fiverr as a place where a person can go and find a service, evaluate the price and delivery time, and then buy a needed service. Many buyers are business owners who need to outsource work on a schedule. If they find a seller and don't know a lot about Fiverr, they may not vet the seller well. If the seller cannot communicate or cannot perform the work, they end up with very late delivery, possibly a poor delivery and they often have to cancel. This is very frustrating for buyers since it can make them late on their own business schedules. Once this happens to a buyer with a poor seller they may not give up on Fiverr but will tend to be a bit cautious with the next purchase. Sometimes this makes buyers a little too trigger-happy with cancellation requests since they fear another bad experience. An excellent seller can get caught off guard when this happens with a new buyer and it's bad for everyone.

As of this writing, Fiverr policy is strict about completion rate, so every cancellation is a problem for a seller. If the seller has less than a 100% completion rate, the Fiverr Editors may become concerned about their service. Of course, sometimes an order must be canceled so the rate isn't always going to be perfect. Even so, Success Managers want sellers to strive for so few cancellations that they have few to no issues with canceling. How can this be done and how can one evaluate the completion rate?

How to Avoid Cancellations:

Step One is to prepare for potential cancellations when you create or edit your gig. Try to really think about how to avoid losing an order while you write your title, description, FAQs and even your requirements. In fact, sometimes the requirements can make a huge difference. Your title should be clear and not describe anything that is misleading. One seller I know of had a gig up in the creative writing category that had this in the title: "I will 'edit proof write spin correct the paper, book, and format.'" Clearly, this was a confusing title in the first place. The reviews on the gig referred to previous purchases for PLR (private label rights) content. PLR is not usually written by the seller but is resold. The gig description advertised original story writing. Altogether, it was all unclear. Did the seller previously sell PLR that buyers were happy with? If so, that may have been done to get some initial reviews for content writing and then switch the gig to a higher paying service with creative writing. The title was entirely ambiguous. A seller who does this kind of thing is going to end up with some unhappy buyers who will ask for a refund.

The FAQs can also help a great deal. If your titles and descriptions are well-written, that's a great start. Then you can use the FAQs to clarify further. Include things like "My services are for background removal and I do not do other Photoshop editing. If I receive an order for editing of an image, I will remove the background and deliver. I do not offer refunds unless I have made an error with the background removal." A buyer who reads this will be less likely to misunderstand the gig or to try to sneak in an order for a more complex photo editing job. This gives the seller the ability to deliver even if it does happen and prevents most buyers from making a mistake. It's a simple thing, but surprisingly few sellers use FAQs this way.

In the gig requirements, you are already past the order point but you may have able to reinforce your policies. A requirement might say "Please tell me the topic of your article here. If you do not provide a topic, I will choose a general business topic and deliver. I do not refund based on topic if no topic was provided." Again, surprisingly few sellers utilize their requirements this way but it really can make a difference. If a buyer did make a mistake, they are more likely to write to you and say that they misunderstood your gig and thought it was for proofreading, not topical writing. You may be able to work out an arrangement to proofread for them, to outsource proofreading and still keep the sale intact, etc.

When you handle an order and there is a sign of a potential dispute or an actual dispute, keep your emotions in check. If you realize you might type something that could cause more problems than it's worth, take a break from the computer. Go for a walk. Binge some Netflix. Come back when you are ready to handle the situation as carefully as possible even if you know you are in the right and the buyer is in the wrong. This doesn't mean that you let a buyer walk over you or that you do many hours of work that you shouldn't have to do. It does mean that you may have to do a balancing act to avoid a cancellation or a bad review. You can learn from the situation and find ways to adjust your gig description and FAQ's to prevent future problems.

Even if you think a buyer is taking advantage of you on purpose, don't say this. If it's true, eventually you will either work it out anyway or cancel. There is no point in being right just for the sake of "winning" an argument. In business, sometimes it's better to vent about these things to a friend or partner later. In the meantime, maintain the professional relationship if possible and you can block the buyer post-review if you need to. See if there is a way you can come to an agreement without putting in so much work that it isn't worth it. If you just can't come to an agreement, take a step away again and give it some thought. If you haven't had any lowered reviews in ages, your completion rate is 100% and you have more orders coming in, it may be worth it to stay polite but to offer a refund to that buyer. Take the "ding" on your record, block the buyer and learn. If you have had recent cancellations, lowered reviews or if you aren't getting many orders to shift things back in your direction, it might be worth it to you to go overboard for the one buyer.

If so, just do whatever it takes to make that buyer happy and keep writing in a positive way no matter how annoyed you feel. When you are done you can still block the buyer so that they cannot order again. It will just be that one order and you'll be done. Learn from the experience and see if you could have missed a red flag or if you could have written something into your FAQs to prevent the issue.

How do you evaluate your completion rate?

1.) Gather Data

Go to Selling > Earnings.
if the current date is the 1st of March, you'll need data from the previous two months. Use the filter to get the data for January and February.

2.) Calculations

Count the orders that show "Canceled Payment Refunded to Buyer".
Count your Order Revenue. That will help you get your Completed Orders.

Add up those two to get a total number of orders you had in the last 60 days, which will be later used to calculate your completion rate.

3.) Calculating your Completion Rate in the last 60 days

Use this formula:

X = All Orders = Canceled Orders + Completed Orders in the last 60 days.
Y = Complete Orders only.

<u>Now you'll follow this:</u>

$$\frac{Y * 100}{X} = \text{Completion rate}$$

<u>To restate this:</u>

Use Y (Completed Orders alone) and multiply by 100, then divide by X (All Orders including Completed and Canceled.)

Example:

From January to February you had 45 Completed Orders and 2 Cancelled Orders. A total number of your orders is 47 (X).

Your rate will be 45*100/47= 95.7%, which will be shown on your profile as your completion rate.

Summary/Takeaways:

- **Success Managers prefer Orders Completed at 99% or higher**
- **The Completion Rate must be over 90% to avoid demotion**

Success Managers recommend that to be evaluated well, you need to offer unique services and maintain a great response rate. What does this really mean to a seller?

Unique

When Fiverr was very young, new gigs often popped up and some had original ideas that couldn't be purchased from another seller on Fiverr. Sometimes they were unique on the entire internet! I fondly recall a seller named madmoo who had the idea to create things out of letters. She might spell something out for someone with paper cutout letters or even Scrabble tiles. She would write out a business name or a Happy Birthday message and then photograph the creative result. It was simple but very unique.

The gig sold very well at even at $5 per gig, she could sometimes make $4 profit in a few minutes. It added up well for her for some time. Eventually, others came along and began to copy what she was doing. Some came up with flashier gig images or added music. The service wasn't entirely unique anymore, but due to her high ranking and TRS badge, she was able to profit from the gig even after other sellers were doing it too. There was still a form of uniqueness in being the first to do it and having more reviews than anyone else.

With Fiverr today, it is very difficult to come up with an idea that is entirely unique. I don't even think this is what Success Managers mean by suggesting that you provide unique work since it is so hard. Like the seller I mentioned above, though, there are ways to continue to stand above the crowd when you have competition. There are also ways to beat out "old" sellers who had a unique service but aren't putting in the same effort anymore. Being unique can mean having the best and most original gig images, a beautifully written profile, an excellent profile image that showcases who you are and what you sell, and so on. Being unique also means making your deliveries stand out.

I sell on Etsy, eBay and other retail sites in addition to my Fiverr work. My first retail experience was with eBay and it was way back when eBay was new. At the time, you could make really good money on eBay with cheap prices and interesting products. You didn't have to put a lot of effort into packaging or flashiness as long as you delivered what you promised and packaged things securely.

For me, eBay hasn't changed all that much except for competition. You need higher quality items, new items, or ultra-low prices to be competitive. Overall, though, you can still slap an item in some quality bubble wrap and stick it in the mail and you are good to go on a good delivery. When I started to sell on Etsy I was selling but I wasn't getting reviews. I was packing items just like I did on eBay. I found that I could command higher prices on Etsy since I sold a lot of hand-made items.

Eventually, I learned that Etsy shoppers expect something a bit different. They love to get their items shipped in a pretty package, get a free extra shiny item and a personal handwritten note goes a LONG way. The Etsy sellers that do the best are the ones that stand out the most in their delivery, not just the items they sell. If they also have great photos of their products and artful descriptions, even better. In the same way, sellers on Fiverr can stand out with the best gig images and personable profile pictures. It's also important to build relationships with your clients, not as personal friends but in a personal way as a business owner.

Response Time and Rate

Response time itself just refers to how quickly you respond to messages on average. While we are on that topic, though, it's important to know that you must answer all messages within 24 hours or you can be demoted for failing to maintain your response *rate* which can be confusing. Note that this only applies to the first message a buyer or potential buyer sends. You don't have to write a string of endless replies, just be quick with your first response. The response might be as simple as "Thank you, I'll be in touch!" but it contributes to your statistics. It's also good to respond to every message even if the message is nonsense or spam.

Fiverr is supposed to filter out spam, but there have been cases where something gets through. You'll receive a message that says that it's been marked as spam and won't count against you, or you'll get a message saying that if you report a message as spam it won't count against you. Go ahead and respond even if you don't have to. If the message is really spam or scam, just say "Reported" and then click report. While Support will correct your response rate if it's truly wrong, it's easier to save yourself the trouble of contacting Support and risking a misunderstanding.

What if you get a message that says a message has been marked as spam and you can't "unspam" it? Here is a little tip. If you can click on the message, you can flip some toggles on your inbox to make sure it counts as a response. Try using "unmark as spam" first and respond, then re-mark it as spam. If that fails, try marking a message as "read" and then "unread" which will sometimes unlock it so that you can send a response. You should also check your archive folder daily since Fiverr sometimes archives message that it considers spam, but they may be real or they may need a response. If you really cannot respond or if the user has been banned, keep an eye on your response rate. If it goes down, take screenshots to prove what happened and send them to Support. That way you can maintain a 100% response rate at all times. If you ever have an unforeseen issue like a power outage or family emergency, you'll be glad you were at 100% since you can afford to lose some of that percentage and still not be demoted.

Summary/Takeaways:

- **Success Managers recommend that you remain as "unique" as possible, which realistically just means to stand out from the crowd**

somewhat.
- You must respond to all messages within 24 hours
- Your response rate should be reasonably good overall. If you just want to earn good money, this could probably be up to 8 hours or even longer, though not usually more than 12. If you want to catch the eye of the Fiverr Editors, you need a response rate of 2 hours or less, preferably even 1 hour.

CHAPTER ELEVEN

Gig Requirements

Success Managers recommend that you really work on your gig requirements. Some people worry that they should have very simple requirements and perhaps ask only one or two questions in the requirements. I've found that many buyers would prefer to see a thorough form to fill out if it means the communication is improved by doing so. You don't have to make all those requirement fields mandatory and in fact, you shouldn't unless there is a good reason to do so. Use the most important fields to ask the critical questions and deliver information. Make those requirements mandatory.

Write up several more questions that help flesh out the buyer's concept. You don't have to make those mandatory, but mention what you want to know and why. Buyers will skip as needed and fill in the rest. (You can write [optional] as needed if that helps.) If it makes things more simple for the buyer, make use of drop-down boxes, attachment fields, etc. Just be thorough so that you have all the information. If you write your requirements carefully enough and make the mandatory sections easiest to fill out you will rarely have a clock running and not enough info to move forward.

Where possible, build in statements to tell the buyer what you will do if they don't fill out a requirement. You can say something like "If you don't tell me what mascot you want in your banner, I will choose a mascot from my library. You are welcome to request a revision if needed." This helps ensure that a buyer won't leave a field blank thinking they can do it later. This helps you if you have to explain to Support what you delivered and why you did it that way. It informs the buyer and protects you.

If you do get the clock started without enough information, quickly write to the buyer. Ask for a time extension in case there are communication issues. Repeat your requirements in different words in case the buyer did not understand. Do everything you can to get the information you need to send a quality delivery and if you have to send a delivery with your choices instead of the buyer's choices, put your intentions in writing so it doesn't count as an empty or partial delivery.

Summary/Takeaways:

- **Make sure that your gig requirements are complete, clear, and request everything needed to start any order.**

When it comes to delivery, a Success Manager would advise you to deliver original high-quality work and to make sure your samples are yours and are good samples. This might seem obvious as advice, but many sellers really don't do it as well as they should. I've seen logo designers who are starting out and assume that it's fine to take a logo from the web and change it up a little. They might make the case that "there is nothing new under the sun" and that even Shakespeare used other sources as inspiration. That's probably true, but there is a big difference in getting inspiration from somewhere and copying something. There is also a big difference between understanding that curved lines will be part of most logos and thinking that you can copy the exact curved lines that make the face of an animal in a corporate logo.

Fiverr wants you to create your own gig images from scratch and to create sample materials that showcase your skills. If you are a writer, write some articles just as sample work. Don't use work you've sold to other clients since that violates their copyright. If you design flyers, make some flyers for fictional events and use your own color choices and designs. This will accurately demonstrate to a buyer what YOUR work will look like. When you do this correctly you will be unique and you will end up with far fewer problems. Buyers will leave more reviews and they will be more descriptive in reviews. You will have fewer cancellations and other disputes.

No matter what you sell:

- Use high resolution in images when applicable
- Use high-quality sound when applicable
- Make your content clear and readable
- Fix typos, spelling errors and grammar issues
- Write in coherent English. You don't have to be perfect, but you should be reasonably fluent.
- Double-check all your work to keep it free of errors, artifacts, and

problems that might cause a buyer to request a revision, cancel, or leave a bad review.

Summary/Takeaways:

- **Deliver unique work that has not been taken from other sources**
- **Make sure that your sample work is yours, is good, and that your deliveries match the quality of the samples**
- **Deliver work with quality resolution, clear sound, good communication, etc.**

Warning: Some sellers make a simple mistake with gig images. When you know the type of work you are capable of and you are making a new gig, it can be tempting to use gig images that you created quickly or to use royalty-free images from the web. It gets your gig up faster and you may feel confident that you can deliver with the same quality. Even if you can deliver the same or better quality, don't fall for this trap. If you use something that appears to be copied you can lose the gig even after it has reviews on it. It only takes one report or one complaint to get you in trouble. Fiverr can deny your gig or worse if your samples are not as they should be. This is true even if your actual deliveries are original and high-quality.

CHAPTER TWELVE

Communication

When you communicate with your clients, a Success Manager would remind you that you run your own business on Fiverr and you must be professional and learn to communicate well in English. Take care that you are friendly with your buyers, but not overly personal. Don't refer to buyers by gender (Ma'am, Sir, Bro) since it is inappropriate and you might be incorrect. Don't refer to buyers by terms that are culturally appropriate for you but might not be elsewhere. A good example of this is the word "dear." In many cultures, it is common and proper to refer to a business customer as "dear." In other countries, this term is only used by someone who is your elder and/or is a relative. If you aren't sure about a word don't use it. Refer to your clients by their usernames or their names IF they sign with that name.

It is also a mistake to call a buyer "friend," "buddy," "Ma," or anything else that could be considered personal. Some buyers won't care and might even like it. Many buyers will find it unprofessional or even offensive. If you offend a buyer and they report you, Fiverr may think that you were trying to insult the buyer. This can get you warned, demoted or banned.

If your English isn't up to par, get in some English-speaking online chat rooms, take an English course with a teacher who is a native speaker or find other ways to improve. Even watching movies and television can help up to a point. If you confuse a buyer or they feel you don't understand what they ask you, you can lose that buyer or get a negative review that affects your future work.

Summary/Takeaways:

Make sure that your communication with everyone on Fiverr is:

- **Clear**
- **Professional**
- **Friendly, but not overly personal**

Warning: **Always rein in your emotions when working with clients. This is a business skill that is a necessity. Sometimes you will feel angry, offended or hurt by something a buyer says or does. You may even be right and some buyers are not nice. (Most are!) No matter what, though, stay professional and polite. It will pay off in the long run. If you need to take a break and go exercise, punch a pillow, drink a calming cup of tea - do it! You might get away with being rude to a buyer who was rude to you since it might have been their fault. If a Fiverr staff member sees your communications, though, you stand a chance of getting in major trouble for being unprofessional no matter what the buyer said to you.**

This does NOT mean that you should continue working for an abusive buyer or ignore what they do. It just means that you don't need to react to the buyer or let them know that they got to you. Report the behavior to Customer Support, especially if it is abusive. Support *does* ban buyers if there is a big enough problem.

Much is said on the Fiverr forum, the Fiverr subreddit and elsewhere about Fiverr Customer Support. People complain about Support and they want to be treated with respect even if they turn out to be in the wrong. This is understandable and we have to try to remember that Support agents are only human. That said, a Success Manager would tell you to think about how you want to be treated and do it even better with your own clients! Why should you? Two reasons:

- It benefits YOU even more than it does Fiverr. You get 80% of the funds the buyer pays (not counting service fees.)
- It benefits Fiverr which makes the Editors more likely to consider you for a promotion, badge or title. Ultimately, this is still to your benefit!

When you work with people who have purchased services from you, they are *your* clients for the duration of your arrangement. I know of many buyers who find one seller they really like for a particular service and they never use any other seller for that service. Those buyers are the clients of the seller even more than they are Fiverr's clients since they will become repeat customers. So, whether you are dealing with a one-time buyer or a repeat client, every communication you have with them represents your own Customer Service. You are a Customer Support agent and a business owner to your client.

If a client comes to you with a problem and you realize the issue isn't your fault, it's very tempting to tell the client that you can't do anything to help them. If the truth is that you can help them in some way, it is often in your best interest to do so.

I can recall one of the best experiences I ever had with a company. I was stranded during a cold Texas winter. I was in a parking garage late at night and it was very frightening. My car wouldn't start and I thought it might be the battery but I wasn't sure. I had jumper cables but no one was around and I was nervous that if someone did come along it might not be a good person. Parking garages can be dangerous places late at night, especially in isolated environments. At the time I had no roadside assistance and I wasn't sure what to do since it was late. I had a card for a tow service in my wallet.

It was a local company and I didn't think I needed a tow, but I had no better ideas at the moment. I called them. They said they would send someone just to see what was going on and that I wasn't obligated to have the car towed. I got back in my car and sat in the cold, unable to run the engine and use the heater. A short time later a tow truck arrived. The company had sent a man and a woman together which comforted me since I felt much less alone and scared! Not only that, they had a thermos of hot coffee! They offered me a hot drink while they took a look at my car. It took them just a few minutes to charge the battery and they didn't let me pay them anything. They wished me a happy holiday season and gave me another card. I knew that I would recommend them to everyone I knew.

I tell this story because I had an issue that night and it wasn't the fault of the tow company. They didn't have to do anything except come out and tell me what it would cost to tow my car and leave me stuck with a tough and expensive decision. Instead, they made me feel safe. They tended to my needs even though they had no obligation. They didn't even charge me. It was the best customer service I had ever received from a company without even hiring them to do anything! Later on, I went to work for the local university and one of my jobs was to have cars towed from the university lot if they had no parking sticker. I always used the tow company that had helped me and it brought them a ton of business. They were always nice to people and helped out if they saw someone in trouble on campus. I'm sure they continued to get more business from other people. A one-time customer service opportunity combined with kindness helped them to become the most popular service in town.

When you have a good client and you go a little bit out of your way to help them even if you don't have to, you will benefit. Many buyers tell other business people about their Fiverr experiences. Others just become repeat customers. They tend to leave great reviews which helps you get even more buyers. Buyers can also leave private feedback about their experiences with you on Fiverr. By going out of your way a little bit, you may catch the attention of the Fiverr Editors. This isn't to say that you should always go super-far for everyone who contacts you or give out free work to everyone who messages you. Those aren't always wise choices. It just means that good customer service goes a long way.

Summary/Takeaways:

- **Provide excellent Buyer Support to your Clients**
- **Work with Unsatisfied Clients to Resolve Issues**

Note: If you have a problem with a Buyer and either Seller or Buyer contacts Support, they will often tell both parties to try to resolve it together first. By developing a habit of providing resolutions for issues when possible, you'll be prepared to do that and come out looking good.

CHAPTER THIRTEEN

Can you get a Success Manager?

Right now there is no guarantee that you will get your own Success Manager no matter what you do. At the time of this writing, though, you can apply for a Success Manager through a lightly publicized survey that Fiverr has listed. (Active May of 2017) To see if it is still active, go to The Fiverr Success Program and Pro Application: http://fiverrsuccess.questionpro.com/?custom1=ed <a href="#BookMark"</a>

Please note: When this link was first publicized, the Fiver Pro program was probably planned by Fiverr staff, but it wasn't in use yet and there was no such thing as a Pro badge or a Pro gig. Even though the Pro program is now in place, what many people don't know is that Fiverr wants more Pros and is willing to groom certain sellers even if they can't get a Fiverr Pro badge yet. Top Rated Sellers sometimes get an advantage in this grooming process, but even level one and level two sellers have a good shot. You can fill out the Pro application no matter what. If you are rejected for Pro (most people are the first time and it takes a while to hear back) you may be selected to get a Success Manager and/or to be watched for closely for promotion to TRS.

If the link above doesn't work when you read this book, don't panic. It still worked as of January 2019, but even if they remove it, just ask on the Fiverr official forum for information about Success Managers or about how to apply for the Pro program. You are also strongly encouraged to write to Fiverr Customer Support. Use something like this as a plan:

- If you are level 0-2 and don't have a strong social media presence, write to

Support anyway, but read these caveats.

- If you are level 0-2 and have worked with some bigger companies or influencers (on or off Fiverr)be sure to tell Support anything you can. If possible, show evidence and get a recommendation letter from one or more of your previous clients. If you can't do that, at least elaborate on your past success.

- Ask Support to consider assigning a Success Manager to your account. They ARE looking for sellers that have potential and you have nothing to lose by asking! It could be your path to a TRS account or if you are already a TRS (or can just skip it) to a Pro badge!

Important: **No matter what - be sure to read a few more pages because it's important to realize that you may NOT need a Success Manager at all!**

If you skipped ahead to see this info, feel free to head back for the rest of the Success Manager in a Box Guide.

What is the Success Management Team (in the Words of a Fiverr Staff Member):

"The Success Management / Seller Success team is assigned here and there to help users improve their offerings on Fiverr. The intention is good, but it can come off as confusing since not everyone has access to a Success Manager and not everyone does things in exactly the same way."

Sometimes Success Managers don't get things right, so don't expect perfection. You aren't perfect and neither are they. You may not even really need one to excel on Fiverr, but if you hear something has been said remember that staff has admitted that Success Managers haven't always worded things as well as they could be.

CHAPTER FOURTEEN

Do you <u>Need</u> a Success Manager?

Do you REALLY Need a Success Manager?

<u>What are the perks?</u>

As of this writing, Success Managers do give their contact info to sellers they are assigned to. This doesn't mean you have instant access to them. What they give out is typically email and Skype or Slack info. You may be able to arrange calls with them and you can send them personal messages via chat/email.

Potentially there is enhanced support for sellers with a Success Manager. They usually suggest that their sellers get in touch if they need anything including things that might normally go through the ticket system.

At one time there was a specialized private forum area for sellers with Success Managers. Not many sellers or SM's were active in that forum area and as far as I know, it was later either disbanded or turned into a Pro Forum. Fiverr would probably consider creating another private forum if it were needed.

Reality:

Sellers who have talked with me about having an SM have said that the experience wasn't quite as great as they hoped.

The first sellers who had SM's got a great deal of helpful information. As far as I know, 90% of that info (if not more) has been reprinted in this book and is now available to any seller who wants to make use of it.

Many sellers who have Success Managers have reported that information was lacking after the first emails and other communications that were sent to those sellers. SM's have not been as consistent about staying in touch as some sellers hoped they would. In some cases, sellers have had to submit tickets through the regular Support system to get assistance with issues. Other than the information that was handed out (and is in this book) the later benefits seem to be minimal.

As of this writing, SM's are sometimes available to speak at public events. If you are a seller that lives in a big area where community events can be held with good attendance, an SM might be willing to come and answer questions. The chance are greater if the seller hosting the event has their own Success Manager.

It is not known if the SM program will continue into mid-2019 and beyond or whether it will be only available to sellers with a Pro badge.

About the Author

Maddie Green (AKA Maddie "FontHaunt") is a freelance writer, researcher, ghostwriter, and pet specialist. She has a BA degree in English, and 2 years of study in Animal Science. She lives in Texas where she loves to hang out with her family and cats, ride horses, garden, provide freelance services, read fiction and non-fiction and of course - write and learn every single day!

Sign up for her mailing list to get more information about upcoming titles!
https://realbeyourself.weebly.com/get-in-touch.html

Find Maddie on:

https://www.fiverr.com/fonthaunt
https://realbeyourself.weebly.com
https://stormyventure.com/
https://petarticle.weebly.com/
https://www.youtube.com/channel/UCxU-ww5kULo8yluBiuH290g

www.amazon.com/author/maddiegreen

Other Books and Resources of Interest:

Maddie currently writes non-fiction on business/ freelancing, pet and animal topics. She also writes fiction in genres such as humor, memoir, literary fiction and more. Please see Maddie Green or Maddie "FontHaunt" Green online for more information! Books come from Juniper Publisher and Stormy Ventures.

~~~

We would also like to introduce a recently released Stormy Ventures book for fans of suspense, historical fiction based on true stories, history, and romance. Please check out the new book:

Airmail to Texas: 8,422 Miles from Home
By Linda Ann

You can find Airmail to Texas in e-book and print on Amazon.com. Linda Ann is an exciting talent showcasing a wonderful story based on a set of secret letters that was hidden away for more than 70 years! Linda Ann is also available for local speaking engagements in Texas. (See contact information below.)

You can contact Linda Ann at jclc3848@sbcglobal.net for more information on display of artifacts and photographs from the 19th-21st century. She can attend book clubs and other events to speak on her books or on historical events, particularly those surrounding World War II. She provides mentoring to those working on memoirs. She also does photo restoration on old family or commercial photographs.

~~~

If you enjoyed the Fiverr Success book and the Freelancing for Fun and Profit series, you may be interested in checking out ghostwriting services provided by Maddie "FontHaunt" Green. You can hire Maddie for pet-related blog and book services and specialty ghostwriting. Maddie also works with individual writers locally in Texas near the Stormy Venture publisher area. If you are interested in Merch related to Freelancing, Pets/Animals or the Real BeYourself Blog, Maddie can help!

You can contact Maddie at realbeyourself@gmail.com for more information.

~~~

In Maddie's fiction, medical consultation was handled by Dr. Isabel Molina of Lamesa, Texas. Dr. Molina is a pioneer for the subscription-based financing model for health care in the Lamesa region. Check out her site at:
http://www.isabelmolinafamilymedicine.com/

~~~

Photography for Stormy Venture and Juniper Publisher books is handled by Susan Zellars, an expert photographer from Odessa, Texas.

www.suezsphotography.com

www.ingramcontent.com/pod-product-compliance
Lightning Source LLC
Chambersburg PA
CBHW030651220526
45463CB00005B/1722